GERRY ANDERSON COLLECTABLES

Rob Burman

AMBERLEY

Many thanks to Vectis Auctions for access to their incredible image archives and for providing the photographs.

First published 2015

Amberley Publishing
The Hill, Stroud
Gloucestershire, GL5 4EP

www.amberley-books.com

Copyright © Rob Burman, 2015

The right of Rob Burman to be identified as the Author of this work has been asserted in accordance with the Copyrights, Designs and Patents Act 1988.

ISBN 978 1 4456 4872 9 (print)
ISBN 978 1 4456 4873 6 (ebook)

British Library Cataloguing in Publication Data.
A catalogue record for this book is available from the British Library.

Typeset in 10pt on 13pt Celeste.
Typesetting by Amberley Publishing.
Printed in the UK.

The Adventures of Twizzle (1957–59)

Our journey into the world of Gerry Anderson collectables begins way back in 1957 with a little-known television series called *The Adventures of Twizzle*. This was the first show to be made by Anderson and featured the first of the puppet-based action that he would become so well known for. The series centred around the titular Twizzle, a doll that resembles a pixie and can magically extend his arms and legs. After escaping from a horrible little girl called Sally – who tried to buy Twizzle for just two shillings from a toy shop – Twizzle teams up with a black cat called Footso, whose paws are so large he clumsily trips over them. The pair travel around saving other unfortunate toys – normally using Twizzle's magical powers – before setting up a safe haven for their friends called Stray Town.

Compared to Anderson's later projects, the animation in *The Adventures of Twizzle* is crude, with no facial expressions on the characters and fairly simple movements. However, that didn't stop Anderson adding some innovative methods, such as a large bridge above the studio floor that allowed the puppeteers to move the puppets without leaning over a backdrop. This allowed the team to use more complicated 3D sets and avoided unsightly shadows from the puppeteers being cast over the characters.

It's a shame that despite *Twizzle* marking the start of Anderson's career, toys are in short supply.

Pelham Puppets Twizzle

Sadly, despite the fact that *The Adventures of Twizzle* is now a significant point in Gerry Anderson's career, it's not a particularly significant point in the history of Gerry Anderson toys. Although the 1950s were considered a 'golden age' for toy manufacturing, with the likes of Corgi Toys and Dinky Toys kicking their diecast production into overdrive, licensed products based on children's television shows weren't particularly popular.

The result is that Twizzle toys are, sadly, almost non-existent. One of the only collectables based on the show was a Twizzle puppet by Pelham Puppets. However, throughout this guide we'll be coming across the name of Pelham Puppets time and time again, so it seems only appropriate to give a little history about that company too.

Despite later being known as Pelham Puppets, when the firm was originally founded in 1947 by Bob Pelham it was called Wonky Toys Ltd in reference to his Second World War nickname of 'The Wonky Donkey Officer', which came about as he would often make small toy donkeys that moved due to a small spring inside them. Wonky Toys opened for business in an office based at Victoria House, Marlborough.

At the time, marionettes were seen as something that professional puppeteers would use, rather than children, so Pelham wanted to create a professional-looking puppet that could easily be used by children. The result was the first ever Pelham Puppets marionette, called Sandy Macboozle – a cheerful-looking Scot clutching a bottle of beer. No need to worry about political correctness in 1947! Macboozle was a success and the company name was changed to Pelham Puppets in 1948.

From there Pelham's success soared and led to the establishment of a special Pelham Puppets club and newsletter called *Pelpup News*. The 1950s saw further expansion with the introduction of Disney characters such as Pluto, Pinocchio and Donald Duck into the range. However, the year we're interested in here is 1957 because that's when the Twizzle puppet was introduced. Although the puppet doesn't have the extendable legs and arms from the show, he still has his recognisable green hat and pixie-like appearance. In terms of value, a Twizzle puppet in its original box was sold at Vectis Auctions for £90, but unboxed examples regularly sell for less than this.

Apart from that, Twizzle toys are very scarce. Your only other options for Twizzle collectables are a series of card games, created by an unknown British manufacturer, featuring characters from the show and an *Adventures of Twizzle* annual from 1958. The latter is the more valuable, with prices pegged at around the £65 mark.

Torchy the Battery Boy (1960/61)

Gerry Anderson's next project once again explored the idea of dolls that were alive but, instead of a character with extendable limbs, this time our hero has a magical torch in his head that can locate lost items – very handy when you can't find your car keys! After Torchy's creator, Mr Bumbledrop, makes the little doll a special cardboard rocket, he jets off into outer space and discovers Topsy Turvy Land – a place where toys come alive! Torchy and his pals create Frutown, in which all the houses are made of giant fruit. Occasionally Torchy and a toy poodle called Pom-Pom journey back to Earth to help out Mr Bumbledrop and teach naughty children how to behave!

With the success of *Twizzle*, Gerry Anderson and the *Torchy* team were keen to advance their puppet techniques again and *Torchy* featured puppets that could open their mouth and move their eyes. Once more the sets were improved, ensuring that in *Torchy* it really did seem like the toys had some to life. The show also featured one of Anderson's most ambitious scenes yet – the opening credits showing Torchy's rocket blasting off into space. The rocket had been rigged with sparklers and a pulley system would pull it towards the sky. However, Anderson became so impatient he plugged the trigger mechanism straight into a normal socket and the whole thing almost exploded ... luckily, they had managed to film the perfect shot.

Pelham Puppets returned with a new marionette inspired by Torchy ... but without that magical torch on his head.

Pelham Puppets Torchy the Battery Boy

For *Torchy the Battery Boy* collectables, we once again have to turn to Pelham Puppets because Torchy toys were in very short supply ... ironic really, considering the show was all about toys that come to life. The Pelham Puppets version features Torchy in a little red jacket with green trousers and a simple replica of that famous magic torch that, sadly, doesn't light up. The Pelham Puppets replica has a slightly less menacing looking face than the real version of Torchy though! Torchy puppets are uncommon, particularly in their boxes, so keep an eye out at toy fairs or car boots because you never know when one might turn up.

Four Feather Falls (1960)

After looking to dolls for the inspiration for previous projects, Gerry Anderson turned his attentions to something a little more realistic for his next idea. The late 1950s had seen a dramatic rise in the popularity of Wild West shows such as *Wagon Train* and *Gunsmoke*, so composer Barry Gray – who had worked with Anderson on *Twizzle* and *Torchy* – suggested a series based around the adventures of a cowboy.

Set in a town called Four Feather Falls, Kansas, towards the end of the nineteenth century, the series centred around the sheriff Tex Tucker. Although the programme was more realistic than *Twizzle* or *Torchy*, there were some fantasy elements to ensure it stood out from typical Wild West shows. You see, after saving a starving Indian boy, Tex is given four magical features. Two allow his dog Dusty and horse Rocky to speak, while the other two allow his guns to magically shoot of their own accord. The latter magical ability was a masterstroke because the often ponderous nature of puppet movement would have restricted Tex's ability to draw and shoot his guns quickly. A pair of magical guns that could shoot on their own removed this potential problem.

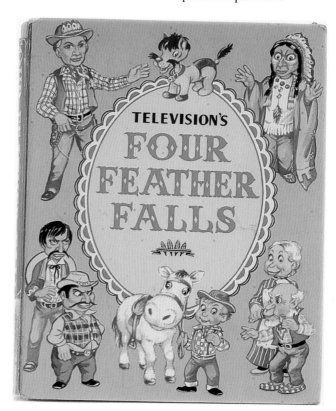

Four Feather Falls featured an unusual cast of Wild West-inspired characters, as seen on the cover of this book.

Compared to Anderson's previous work, *Four Feather Falls* was exceptionally ambitious with huge, detailed sets to create the feeling of a living, breathing Western town. However, *Four Feather Falls* was also important as it provided the foundations of Anderson's famous Supermarionation technique for creating realistic puppet movement. The voiceovers for *Four Feather Falls* – including work by Nicholas Parsons, who provided the voice for Tex – were recorded separately before filming had begun. Now this is where it gets a bit clever: the recorded voiceovers were then used to create electronic pulses that were sent down the metal wires used to operate the mouth of the puppet. By selecting the appropriate wire, the current generated just enough electricity to move the mechanism in the jaw, creating the impression that the character was talking. Although not as advanced as the later Supermarionation, this was a revolution compared to what had come previously.

Collect the magical feathers in this board game inspired by the classic show.

Bell Toys Four Feather Falls Game

Our best collectable yet is based on *Four Feather Falls* and it's a board game, rather than the more typical puppets we've already seen. The game was created by Bell (Toys & Games) in London, a company that specialised in creating board games inspired by popular television shows at the time. Others games included some based on ITV quiz shows, *Take Your Pick* and *Double Your Money*, along with American series like *Hawkeye* and *Wagon Train*. The *Four Feather Falls* game sees players taking on the role of Grandpa Twink, Jake, Ma Jones or Tex Tucker as they travel around Four Feather Falls collecting feathers. Rather than a dice, the game comes with a colourful card spinner and also includes card feathers, just like the magic ones in the show. Cardboard games, particularly with all their components intact and a decent box, are certainly hard to find now, so when the *Four Feather Falls* game does crop up for sale, you can expect to pay around the £100 mark.

However, if you can't afford that kind of money but still like the idea of getting your own piece of *Four Feather Falls* history, there are some cheaper options available. Something that regularly comes up for grabs is the *Tex Tucker's Four Feather Falls Annual* featuring Tex on the cover riding Rocky and a more general *Four Feather Falls Annual* featuring multiple members of the cast. Even in good

Four Feather Falls saw the number of toys and games produced increased, including these charming jigsaw puzzles.

condition they can be snapped up for around the £20 mark. Then again, not all the books are cheap. The publishers Collins produced a series of activity books – including *Makooya's Painting Book* and *Dusty's Painting Book* – with pictures to colour in and puzzles to complete. Due to the fact many of these books were completed then potentially thrown away, they're in short supply today and sell online for around £40 ... when you can track them down.

Supercar (1961/62)

Gerry Anderson's next work is arguably one of his most significant, not only because it laid the foundations for the important shows of his future career but also because it signified a change in the approach to licensed toy-making. *Supercar* launched in 1961 and Anderson went on to make thirty-nine episodes of this groundbreaking series over the course of the next year. The show told the adventures of Mike Mercury, who piloted the titular Supercar – a vehicle that could fly like a jet as well as travel on land thanks to a cushion of air, rather than wheels, and could even head underwater. Mike was joined by boffins Rudolph Popkiss and Horatio Beaker, along with young boy Jimmy Gibson and his pet monkey, Mitch, at a special laboratory in Black Rock, Nevada. Although most episodes would see Mike Mercury rescuing people or catching villains in his Supercar, he would also occasionally face off against the evil Masterspy, who was determined to destroy the car.

Looking back at *Supercar* now, it's easy to see how it set in stone so many of the Anderson staples that would later become key parts of *Stingray* and *Thunderbirds*. Most significantly, it was the first time that Anderson referred to the ingenious method of puppet control as 'Supermarionation' and the name appeared in the last thirteen episodes of the second series. In fact, the techniques used during *Four Feather Falls* hadn't altered, it was just that the method hadn't been given an official name until now.

Supercar was Anderson's most ambitious project yet and also saw an explosion in licensed toys.

The variety of *Supercar* toys was impressive, like this magnetic picture set that allowed the owner to create their own adventures.

Another element introduced in *Supercar* that would become a key part of Anderson's later work was the introduction of a fantastic vehicle and a spectacular launch sequence. Anderson is quoted as saying the reason he introduced vehicles into his shows was to cut down on the amount of walking required because the puppets always looked a little ungainly while trying to walk. The benefit of a vehicle is that the character could quickly jump in and then zoom around, allowing the audience to suspend their disbelief that little bit more. Meanwhile, the complicated launch sequence was something that had arguably been tested with the rocket blasting off in *Torchy* but here was taken to new heights. Mike would test the engines (with suitably explosive special effects) before opening the roof door and blasting off into the atmosphere.

Budgie Models Supercar

As well as proving a huge turning point for Gerry Anderson, *Supercar* is also a big turning point in toy production because, rather than the typical rather simple puzzles or puppets we've seen before, *Supercar* inspired some fantastic toys that have really stood the test of time. Of course, *Supercar's* futuristic vehicle and high-tech gadgets certainly helped. The late 1950s and early 1960s had seen an explosion in science fiction toys, particularly ray guns and spaceships based on the adventures of Dan Dare, who had been appearing in the pages of *Eagle* comics since 1950. So *Supercar* slotted into this new passion for outer space perfectly, rather than *Four Feather Falls*, which may have seen a little old fashioned in comparison.

Supercar also provided us with our first diecast replica of a Gerry Anderson vehicle – something that would become extremely common in the future. However, the first Anderson diecast vehicle wasn't made by household names Dinky Toys or Corgi Toys; instead it fell to Morestone (also known as Budgie Toys). Morestone was set up in the 1940s as a toy wholesaler distributing the products of other companies, but in 1954 the founders opened up their own die-casting facility. Although Morestone generally released replicas of trucks and commercial vehicles, in the late 1950s and early 1960s it produced a range of toys inspired by the adventures of Noddy. The company made a number of cars, bicycles and even a locomotive bearing the image of the toy with the blue hat.

In 1959 Morestone launched the Budgie Toys range, which came in yellow boxes bearing a little logo of a blue budgie. The Budgie series is where we must look for our first Anderson diecast. Budgie's Supercar replica was produced between 1962 and 1964 and is actually a pretty decent representation of the television vehicle. Finished in red and silver, the Budgie Supercar has a large clear plastic dome for the cockpit, complete with a Mike Mercury figure inside. What's more, just like the 'real' thing, it had retractable wings that slotted into the rear of the car. Unfortunately, although a great play feature, the wings were a very tight fit, meaning the paint is easily scratched off them. In fact, it's almost impossible to extract the wings without chipping or scratching the paint a little. Another part of the model that has a tendency to be damaged is a small plastic grey aerial on the nose. It's extremely delicate and can be snapped off during transport, even when contained in the box.

Another thing to note is that although the Budgie Supercar is invariably seen with a red body and silver detailing, there are also versions with the colours reversed. In this version the retractable wings are silver, rather than red.

Budgie's diecast Supercar is a wonderful little replica, although it has some delicate parts that can easily snap off.

Merit Supercar Intercom Set

Our next toy really shows how technology had advanced in the 1960s, particularly compared to the simple card games for *Twizzle* and *Torchy*. The Merit Super Intercom Set allowed children to pretend they were intrepid adventurers communicating on high-tech walkie talkies. The truth is they were really just glorified tin cans on strings.

Although Merit was the more prominent name on the box, it was actually the brand name for J. & L. Randall Ltd, a British toy manufacturer that created a huge range of toys, from science sets to model railways, before being bought out by Letraset in 1978 for £12.5 million.

The outer box shows Mike Mercury chatting to Popkiss via the device – although they probably didn't have to be within a few metres of each other, like the toy – while the Supercar flies overhead. Inside the box are illustrations of the main characters, along with instructions on how to use the set. Surprisingly though, despite the fact the Intercom dates from 1962 and features such impressive artwork, at auction it can be acquired for under the £100 mark.

Communicate with your friends ... as long as they're almost in the same room, thanks to the Merit Intercom Set.

Remco Toys Supercar Computer Disc Car

While we're on the subject of high-tech toys, here's something that must have been at the cutting edge of toy production in 1962. Created by Hong Kong company Remco, this impressive battery-operated toy had different shaped plastic discs that could be inserted into a lift-up panel at the rear. There were eight different movement patterns, including circles, zig-zags and something called 'dipsy-doodles', depending on which disc was used.

Although the mechanical side of the toy was advanced, the actual toy bears little resemblance to the on-screen Supercar and the paint job is simple to say the least. If you fancy picking up one of these, expect to pay around £100 for an unboxed example.

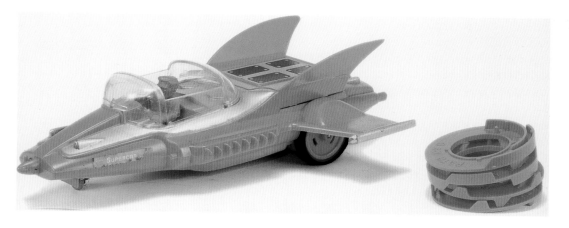

This 'computerised' Supercar must have seemed so high-tech back when it was first released. Even now it's still an impressive model.

Cecil Coleman Supercar Gift Set

For something really rare, you need to track down the Cecil Coleman gift set from 1964 – another product that hails from Hong Kong. The set features not only a plastic version of Supercar, which certainly bears a strong resemblance to the Budgie diecast version, but also plastic figures of Mike Mercury, Jimmy Gibson, Dr Beaker, Mitch the Monkey and Professor Popkiss.

Although the plastic Supercar on its own crops up now and again, finding the set on its original illustrated backing card with the plastic bubble intact is almost impossible. One example did sell at Vectis Auctions in 2009 for £540, but an example was recently spotted online for almost double that. Super indeed!

Plaston Supercar with Retractable Wings

Arguably the most accurate representation of the on-screen Supercar was created by Plaston in 1961. This snap-together set measures more than 30 cm long and even has retractable wings, just like the 'real' thing. The colouring is a little off but in terms of shape, Plaston really pulled this one off perfectly.

Once again though, it's the cracking box that adds the icing to the cake. The front shows an illustration of Supercar blasting out of the water, while the rear shows Mike Mercury, Popkiss and Beaker tinkering with the futuristic vehicle. Value-wise ... well, you could be looking at around the £600 to £800 mark for examples in their box and in good condition, but even unboxed Plaston Supercars can still make hundreds.

Plaston's take on Supercar is among the most rare Gerry Anderson toys.

Louis Marx (Hong Kong) Friction Prototype Supercar

Finally, we'll close our look back at *Supercar* with something truly unique – a Louis Marx friction-powered Supercar. The reason why it's unique is that only one was ever made because the toy never went into production. Measuring 23 cm, the toy came with Mike Mercury and Dr Beaker figures and was put up for sale at Bonhams auction house in 2010. Here's what the auctioneer had to say about it:

> This is the only known example, a licence was granted but it didn't go into production. I can only presume that the Fairylite Supercar hit the shops first and that Marx thought that there would not be sales for two friction drive plastic models of more or less the same dimensions, which is a shame as this toy would have been in every way superior to the Fairylite. The body is closely proportioned there are two nicely moulded figures of Mike Mercury and Dr Beaker and the rear paneled section is clear red plastic so perhaps the production one would have had a 'sparking' motor using flints as a few toys of the time did and so did the later Fairylite Fireball XL5.

Estimated at £1,500 to £2,000, the lot didn't sell, but what a fascinating look at what could have been from Marx.

Supercar was quite the merchandising powerhouse, appearing on everything from lunch boxes to cups.

Bonhams put this unusual 'what-if' Marx Toys Supercar under the hammer but it failed to sell ... where is it now?

Fireball XL5 (1962/63)

After exploring air, sea and land with *Supercar*, Gerry Anderson's next project was certainly his most ambitious yet. *Fireball XL5* was set 100 years into the future (2063) and featured the crew of the Fireball XL5 spaceship and its pilot Steve Zodiac. In a period when humanity had colonised the far reaches of space, Steve protected Sector 25 of the Solar System, at the behest of the World Space Patrol.

Along with Steve, the other members of the crew included Commander Zero, the leader of the World Space Patrol, and his assistant Lieutenant Ninety, Doctor Venus, a female doctor of space medicine, navigator and engineer Matthew Matic and co-pilot Robert the Robot. In a similar vein to Mitch the Monkey from *Supercar*, they were also joined by Zoonie the Lazoon, a telepathic alien pet belonging to Venus. The show saw the team going up against a range of bizarre aliens such as the Subterrans, rescuing stranded pilots and even tackling the imaginatively named Mr and Mrs Space Spy ... not exactly the most inconspicuous of names!

Fireball XL5 featured the spectacular space adventures of Steve Zodiac and his brave crew.

The spaceship XL5 was based at the incredible Space City, which was Anderson's most impressive set yet. Once again, the show opened with a stunning launch sequence which saw XL5 taking off from a huge ramp, complete with blazing afterburners. Anderson actually built several different versions of the ship to use while filming, depending upon the scene. A small one was used for flying scenes in space, while a slightly larger version was used in the launch sequence and a huge 7-foot model was used for close-ups of the ship.

Multiple Toy Makers Steve Zodiac's Fireball XL5 Space City

There is really only one place to start with *Fireball XL5* collectables and that is the magnificent Multiple Toy Makers version of Space City from 1964. This wonderful playset included a 21-inch-long plastic version of XL5 complete with a spring-loaded track that could be used to launch the spaceship. Other accessories included a jet car, jetmobiles, transport truck and trailer, figures of the crew and lots more. In the TV series, the nose cone of Fireball XL5 could detach to form Fireball Junior and that's exactly what happened with the toy too. Another additional element was the inclusion of cardboard buildings that could be used to create a Space City set. Finding these buildings still unpunched on their card is no easy task and certainly adds to the value. An advert from the period states: 'You control launchings and landings from HQ. Hours of fun for the junior astronaut!'

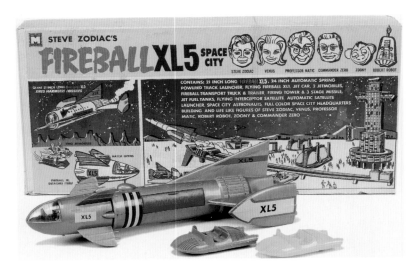

Multiple Toy Maker's Space City set is a delight and, because the parts often go missing, complete examples are extremely sought after.

American company Multiple Toy Makers, also known as MPC, made a huge variety of plastic toys, including figures, model kits and some fantastic James Bond items, such as the 007 Attaché Case. Many pieces of the Space City set – such as the launch tower – were used in other space-themed sets from MPC, including the Apollo Lunar Station and Beyond Tomorrow sets, however there was nothing quite like the original XL5 ship.

Because there are so many pieces in the MPC Space City set, it's exceptionally tricky to find a totally complete example, though they do crop up occasionally. Depending on the condition, they'll fetch around the £500 mark, but that can go up for absolutely pristine examples.

Multiple Toy Makers Galaxy Patrol Set

As well as producing the large Space City set, MPC also released some of the contents as part of the smaller Galaxy Patrol set, which contained figures of Steve Zodiac, Robert the Robot and Zoony along with two jetmobiles, Fireball XL1 launcher and jet car.

The contents were contained in a fairly simple blue cardboard box with cellophane over the front; however, the problem is that the rear of the box featured some 'cut out and keep' Fireball XL5 cards. This meant that most children quickly snipped out the cards and chucked the rest of the box away ensuring that, nowadays, boxed examples are scarce.

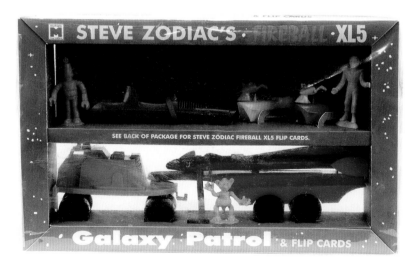

Multiple Toy Makers also released examples featuring just a few models from the Space City Set.

Unfortunately the rear of the pack included 'cut out and keep' figures so intact ones are scarce.

Lyon's Maid Fireball XL5 Kit

Here's something a little bit different. In 1963, Lyon's Maid, the ice cream and ice lolly maker, ran a promotion where those with a sweet tooth could send away for a special Fireball XL5 plastic kit. For just the price of two Zoom ice lolly wrappers and the postage value of 4s 6d a lucky recipient would receive the large kit, measuring more than 30 cm long. Produced by Kitmaster, the XL5 contained fifty parts, glue and a special stand to display the rocket on. Rather amusingly, the advert for the promotion invited children to send their completed cut-out form to Steve Zodiac himself at Glacier House, Hammersmith Grove, London, W6.

To accompany this tie-in, there was also a series of Zoom television adverts produced featuring Steve Zodiac and his glamorous companion Venus. One of the colour adverts shows a Zoom ice lolly blasting off into space while Steve comments: 'Zoom, the new space ice lolly with three fruit flavoured stages and there's a space picture card with every Zoom. Get your Zoom now!'

Actually, this wasn't the first time Anderson and a confectionary company had worked together for an advert. Mike Mercury also

Ice lolly fans could get this Lyon's Maid Fireball XL5 by collecting empty packs of the Zoom lolly.

starred in his own ice cream-themed ad for the Walls threepenny cornet with 'streamlined top'. 'Only thruppence, let's get some more,' exclaims Mike while clutching onto his own uneaten ice cream. It wasn't the last time Anderson characters starred in Lyon's Maid adverts and *Stingray, Thunderbirds* and *Captain Scarlet* all got their own ice lollies, with the Super Seajet, FAB and Orbit respectively.

Fairylite Fireball XL5 Jetmobile

Along with the XL5 itself, another recognisable vehicle from the show was the jetmobile used by Steve and his crew. Anderson had already introduced the Supercar to restrict scenes of the puppets walking awkwardly and now that was taken one step further with the jetmobiles. These flying bikes were used by the team to speed around the sets as much as possible, reducing the amount of time they were actually required to walk around. Think of them as futuristic mobility scooters.

In 1962 Fairylite produced its own take on the jetmobile, complete with Steve Zodiac at the controls and a friction motor to help it zip along. It's an exceptionally rare piece, thanks to the fact that parts like the handlebars or aerials are easily snapped off and you're even more unlikely to find an example in the illustrated box. One did crop up at Vectis Auctions in 2012 and sold for £800, and even that was missing the rear aerial.

However, if you want something exceptionally rare, try to hunt down the same version of the jetmobile but with Venus rather than Steve at the controls. Although the box proudly proclaims 'get the companion model piloted by Venus' it is thought they were uncommon at the time and have now almost become legend, tucked away in private collections or hidden in lofts waiting to be discovered.

Gerry Anderson used jetmobiles in the show to avoid those potentially cumbersome walking scenes featuring the puppets.

Golden Gate Steve Zodiac's Jetmobile

If you still want to get hold of a *Fireball XL5* jetmobile but don't fancy paying top whack, it's worth considering the Golden Gate version of the flying vehicle. This time Steve is joined on the back of the friction-powered jetmobile by his jovial little alien pal Zoonie. The toy isn't actually a bad representation of the pair and even the shape of the futuristic transport is captured well in this plastic replica. However, something to watch out for again is the aerials and handlebars, which are easily snapped off or damaged.

Zoonie joins Steve Zodiac for a ride on his Golden Gate Jetmobile.

Merit Fireball XL5 Rocket Gun

Finally, we'll return to our old friend Merit with the *Fireball XL5* Rocket Gun, complete with two safety rockets with secret message chamber. That's right – as well as shooting Granny, you could send her a message asking for more pocket money at the same time! Genius.

Typically the gun appears without its box, which is a shame because the bright pink packaging, complete with an illustration of a serious-looking Steve Zodiac clutching the weapon, is actually extremely eye-catching. The gun itself is finished in black plastic, while the darts are bright red with black rubber tips.

Rather like the *Supercar* Intercom Set, Merit also used the same mould for a Dan Dare weapon, known as the Rocket Gun. The shape is identical but with Dan Dare branding instead of *Fireball XL5* on the gun, plus it tends to be finished in silver/grey, rather than black.

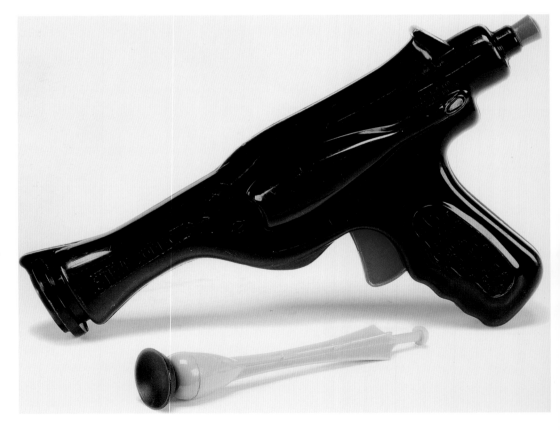

Watch out Granny! Little Tommy's armed with the *Fireball XL5* gun.

Stingray (1964/65)

After venturing into the sea briefly with *Supercar*, Gerry Anderson returned to the waves for his most ambitious project yet – a show in which all the action took place almost entirely underwater. Launched in 1964, *Stingray* was the first Supermarionation show in full colour, ensuring the brightly coloured underwater scenes looked like nothing seen in Anderson's previous work.

In a similar vein to *Fireball XL5*, *Stingray* saw a team of intrepid heroes protecting Earth, but this time they were patrolling the seas rather than outer space. Set two years after *Fireball XL5* in 2065, the plot focuses around the World Aquanaut Security Patrol (WASP) and Captain Troy Tempest, the pilot of the titular *Stingray* submersible.

In the vein already established by Anderson's previous work, Troy was joined by a quirky crew – navigator 'Phones', Commander Samuel Shore, his daughter Lieutenant Atlanta Shore, Sub-Lieutenant John Horatio Fisher and the aquatic Marina, a mute mermaid who provides a love interest for Troy (and who also provided the subject for the memorable closing theme music). The main antagonist against WASP is the evil King Titan and his Aquaphibians, a nation of warrior-like mer-men who are determined to destroy *Stingray*. As part of their campaign to bring an end to *Stingray*, King Titan builds his own combat submarine – a mechanical fish known as the Terror Fish.

Stingray is an absolutely spectacular visual feast and the underwater scenes were like nothing else at the time. Of course, an underwater setting could have caused some issues for the production of the show because moving the puppets in water would have been impossible.

Stingray found a new audience in the early 1990s when repeats were shown on the BBC and Matchbox produced a new range of toys.

The Chad Valley Give-a-Show Projector featured the adventures of Troy Tempest and WASP.

Anderson once again used some great practical innovation to achieve his goal. All the underwater scenes were actually filmed on a normal set but the camera was positioned behind a tank of water containing real fish and air bubbles. The final touch was some special lighting that looked like beams of sunshine coming through the ocean's surface. Even today, when watching *Stingray* it's hard to tell that it wasn't all shot underwater.

Fairylite Scale Model Stingray with Friction Motor

Well, there's only one place we can really begin with *Stingray* toys and that's with *Stingray* itself. In the show, the all-action submarine could travel at more than 300 knots and submerge to depths of more than 36,000 feet – although, sadly, many of the *Stingray* toys weren't waterproof so it's best not to recreate your own Marineville in the bath.

One of the most sought after *Stingray* toys is the Fairylite piece, complete with friction motor to allow it to zip over the carpet. Based in Hong Kong, Fairylite made a huge range of plastic toys, including dolls' house accessories, plastic versions of popular diecast models and a few toys inspired by television icons, such as the Ford Zephyr from *Z Cars* and its own take on *Stingray*.

The toy itself measures 26 cm long and captures the general feel of the original *Stingray* – although the colouring is overly simple compared to the show version. Still, that hasn't stopped it becoming highly collectable and a boxed example in good condition is now worth around the £200 mark.

Fairylite's friction-powered Stingray is among the most sought after Anderson collectables.

Lincoln International Remote Control Stingray

If you fancied something a bit more advanced, Lincoln International's remote control take on *Stingray* would certainly float your boat (pardon the pun). Lincoln International is perhaps a little unusual compared to most of the American, British or Eastern companies we've come across so far because it was actually based in New Zealand – though many of the toys were still made in Hong Kong. The firm was founded in 1946 by Lincoln Laidlaw and produced its first toy in 1948. However, it was really the 1960s that proved to be the golden age for Lincoln as it began to manufacture a huge host of licensed toys, like the super Batman Freezeray Gun, numerous *Noddy in Toyland* vehicles and, of course, some cracking Gerry Anderson-themed products.

Lincoln's remote control *Stingray* is jam-packed with features. The wired remote control allows the model to move forwards and backwards, along with operating lights on the vehicle and a variety of noises, including a horn, whistle and siren.

Technology had come a long way since the days of *Twizzle* – just take a look at this remote controlled *Stingray* from Lincoln International.

Other Stingray models

It's also worth noting some of the other *Stingray* models available – some of which are so rare, it was difficult to find quality pictures of them. Among the rarest is the Plaston *Stingray*. This fairly simple plastic blue and yellow model with silver detailing doesn't look much compared to the Lincoln International example but it's the box that has made this one so rare. You see, the rear of the cardboard pack included 'cut out and keep' models of Troy Tempest and the other members of WASP and, as a result, most children in the 1960s would have gleefully cut the box to bits to get their hands on the simple figures. Sadly this means that perhaps only a handful of boxed examples are in existence today.

Another couple of pieces worthy of mention comes courtesy of Lone Star (a name we shall return to shortly) as it produced two models – one powered by a clockwork motor and the other operated via an elastic band. The latter is actually one of the few *Stingray* toys that can be used in water, thanks to its simple motor.

Lakeside Toys Terror Fish

Of course, if you've got all these *Stingray* models, you really need something for them to battle against and, luckily, Lakeside Toys has just the thing for you in the form of the Aquaphibian Terror Fish. While WASP had *Stingray*, King Titan had a fleet of these gruesome-looking submersibles.

The toy itself is among the best Gerry Anderson-inspired collectables, in this author's opinion. Made from tinplate and measuring just over 20 cm long, when the Terror Fish is pushed along the friction motor also moves the eyes, mouth and tail to create the image of a hideous swimming beast. What's more, Lakeside has absolutely nailed the look of the mechanical creature ... although the television version didn't have quite such googly eyes!

Lakeside also produced a version of *Stingray* which closely resembles the Lincoln International piece – although this one has a friction motor, rather than a battery-powered remote control. A bit like the Terror Fish, when Lakeside's *Stingray* is pushed along certain parts move. The periscope goes up and down and the turbine (known as the Ratemaster) on the back rotates.

Lakeside's fantastic Terror Fish captures the awful look of the on-screen Terror Fish nicely.

Lakeside Toys Stingray Glove Puppets

As well as producing *Stingray* and the Terror Fish, Lakeside also turned its attention to the characters in the show too. However, rather than producing potentially complicated stringed puppets, like those made by Pelham Puppets for Gerry Anderson's other shows, Lakeside went for something a little more straight forward. This included a series of glove puppets featuring Troy Tempest, Titan, an Aquaphibian and Titan's back-stabbing spy X2-Zero. All came in plastic see-through bags with a small card base showing an illustration of the character. The puppets themselves had a cloth body and plastic moulded head.

Strings ... where we're going, we don't need strings! Instead we can just use a hand puppet.

Mettoy Stingray Glove Puppets

However, Lakeside wasn't the only company to make *Stingray* puppets and in 1965 Mettoy (better known as the company behind Corgi diecast cars) released a set of *Stingray* glove puppets featuring Troy Tempest, Phones, Commander Shore and Marina ... a good selection to go against the bad guys from Lakeside. They were made in a similar style to the Lakeside examples with a vinyl head attached to a cloth body.

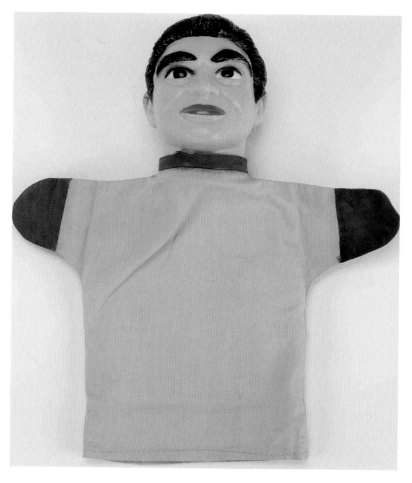

Hand puppets were clearly the in-thing for *Stingray*.

Mettoy's hand puppet series was the perfect companion to the enemies produced by Lakeside.

Lone Star Stingray Gun

Moving on to something rather different now with the Lone Star *Stingray* Gun. Based in north London and started in 1939, Lone Star was the brand name for Die Casting Machine Tools Ltd (DCMT) and it specialised in making diecast vehicles and toy guns. Initially the company made Wild West-inspired toy guns, which were exceedingly popular at the time, but over the years it expanded into licensed products based on James Bond, *The Man from U.N.C.L.E.* and lots more.

One of those licensed guns was inspired by *Stingray*, although it doesn't bear a great deal of resemblance to the guns briefly shown in the series. Finished in bright green with an orange barrel, the Lone Star gun can be used to fire caps – the perfect thing for kids wanting to surprise next door's cat.

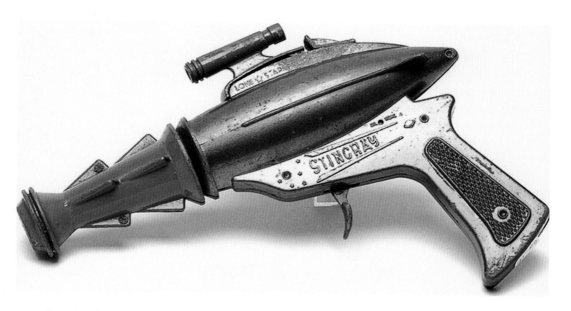

Lone Star's Stingray gun appeared in numerous forms, including Dan Dare and Batman versions.

The reason why it doesn't look like the gun from the show is that Lone Star reused this same mould for numerous guns released around the same time. The first release was a Dan Dare ray gun finished in silver and with 'Dan Dare' written in yellow along the side and another was a Batman-inspired piece in blue with a bat-shaped insignia on the hilt. The Lone Star gun generally tends to turn up without its box, which is a real shame because the box is beautifully illustrated with a picture of Troy Tempest clutching the weapon, with *Stingray* and Marineville HQ in the background. However, even without the box, decent examples are worth around £100.

Morlaine Ltd Stingray Arm Fins

Ever wanted to swim at supersonic speed like Troy and Marina? Perhaps forgetting the fact that supersonic speed is actually 78 mph? That was the claim with these unusual *Stingray* Arm Fins, which not only acted as a swimming aid but supposedly pushed your doggy-paddle to supersonic speeds!

There's a great advert from 1964 promoting these bizarre swimming aids in which Phones and Troy find a huge diamond in the centre of a rock and encounter a school of poisonous fish. 'They won't catch us,' says Phones. 'No, we've got our *Stingray* Arm Fins,' answers Troy. The WASP team then destroys the angry poisonous fish with some missiles. 'Well Marina we're safe again – and we've got the diamond,' boasts Troy back in the safety of *Stingray*. 'Thanks to *Stingray* Arm Fins. They give us such supersonic speed!' laughs Phones.

The fins themselves were made of red plastic and were designed to be slipped onto the user's wrists. A set of four holes in each fin helped the swimmer to glide through the water with ease, as demonstrated by some instructions included with the fins that show Marina gracefully swimming through the sea ... in a dress. Certainly one of the more curious *Stingray* collectables but a lot of fun!

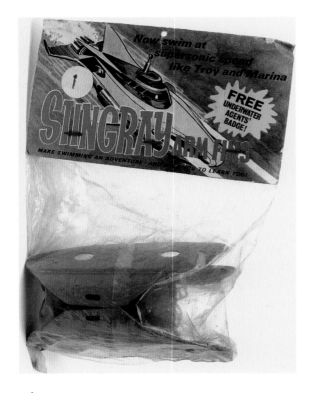

Swim faster than ever with these bizarre *Stingray* Arm Fins.

Thunderbirds (1965/66)

Although Gerry Anderson's previous work had been extremely popular, arguably these shows were dwarfed by the phenomenal global success of his next show: *Thunderbirds*. From the opening booming voice of Peter Dyneley shouting '5 ... 4 ... 3 ... 2 ... 1 ... Thunderbirds are Go!' to the spectacular launch sequences of the different *Thunderbirds* vehicles, the show took everything Anderson had learned from his previous work and turned it up to 11. There were scenes in space like *Fireball XL5*, underwater action with the aquatic Thunderbird 4 like *Stingray* and even a quirky boffin in the shape of Brains, like Popkiss and Beaker in *Supercar*. The only thing really missing was a bizarre sidekick like Mitch the Monkey!

Whereas *Fireball XL5* had the World Space Patrol and *Stingray* featured the World Aquanaut Security Patrol, *Thunderbirds* centered around a secret organisation known as International Rescue. The group was led by millionaire ex-astronaut Jeff Tracy, along with his five sons: Scott, John, Virgil, Gordon and Alan. Each of the boys was allocated a high-tech vehicle: Thunderbird 1 (a silver and blue rocket) piloted by Scott; Thunderbird 2 (the iconic green aircraft that could carry different vehicle pods) was piloted by Virgil; Alan and John shared duties in Thunderbird 3 (a large red spacecraft used mainly for outer space rescues); Thunderbird 4 (a small yellow submarine) was driven by Gordon; and, finally, John and Alan also took duties in Thunderbird 5, a space station in orbit around Earth. These five vehicles – particularly Thunderbird 2 – have become some of the most iconic vehicles to grace the small screen and have inspired countless toys. Meanwhile, International Rescue was also joined by London agent Lady Penelope and her butler Parker. Just like the Tracy Brothers, Penelope had her own high-tech vehicle in the form of FAB1, a six-wheeled Rolls-Royce packed with gadgets, such as hidden machine guns and booby traps.

In terms of plot, special effects and production quality, *Thunderbirds* was really the high point of Anderson's career and the action sequences featuring International Rescue are spectacular. In fact, the budget for each episode was the biggest yet and a typical episode contained around a hundred special effects shots, according to essay writer Jonathan Bignell. An amazing feat when you consider the earlier shows like *Twizzle* and *Torchy*. *Thunderbirds* really did take Gerry Anderson's work to new heights and helped him cross that divide between producing shows for children to making programmes that adults could also enjoy.

Thunderbirds has found worldwide fame, with toy companies around the globe creating their own toys inspired by the show.

Despite the fact that *Thunderbirds* went on to be a worldwide success with fans in far flung places like Japan and America, the second series of the bombastic show only had six episodes. This was after Lew Grade's negotiations to sell the show in America fell through and three US networks (NBC, CBS and ABC) all pulled out of the deal. So, despite having only thirty-two episodes, *Thunderbirds* has arguably become Anderson's most popular work and, ironically, having the second series pulled before its time only added to that sense of greatness, in a similar fashion to other cult programmes like *Fawlty Towers*. The candle that burns brightest, burns half as long, as the saying goes.

Thunderbirds' popularity in Japan also spawned a little known cartoon spin-off called *Thunderbirds 2086*, set twenty years after the original series. First broadcast in 1982, the number of vehicles was expanded to seventeen and although some were based on the ones seen in Anderson's work, others were completely new, like the huge Thunderbird 17 which could fit all the other vehicles, apart from Thunderbird 6, inside. Sadly no toys were ever produced for *Thunderbirds 2086* and even the show had fairly limited success, which meant not all the episodes were broadcast.

Finally, we come back up to date because, in 2015, *Thunderbirds* has made a spectacular return in the form of *Thunderbirds Are Go!*

Lady Penelope's glamorous appearance ensured there are plenty of toys and games bearing her image.

Gone are the clunky but loveable puppets and in comes some slick computer-generated characters and vehicles. With a new series of toys being produced, *Thunderbirds* could be about to find a whole new audience and yet another generation will fall in love with the adventures of the Tracy Brothers.

Dinky Toys

For *Thunderbirds* toys there's really only one place to start and that's at Dinky's Binns Road factory up in Liverpool. Dinky was developed by Frank Hornby, the serial toy inventor who had launched Meccano, under the name Mechanics Made Easy, in 1901. The huge success of the construction toy led to Hornby releasing his first tinplate trains in 1927 and in 1931 it was decided that a set of vehicles would be the perfect accessory to accompany these wonderfully detailed locomotives. The initial set of vehicles were released as 'Modelled Miniatures' and included six vehicles: a sports car, sports coupé, truck, delivery van, farm tractor and tank.

According to the *Ramsay's British Diecast Catalogue*, around this time American company Tootsie Toys had started exporting model vehicles to the UK and they were proving to be very popular. Seeing the success of Tootsie, Meccano Ltd decided to expand its offerings and 'Modelled Miniatures' became 'Meccano Dinky Toys'. Then in 1934 the 'Meccano' part of the branding was dropped and the range became known as just 'Dinky Toys'.

Up until 1967, Dinky Toys had tended to stick to producing only 'real' vehicles such as road cars, planes and trucks, but that all changed with the release of diecast versions of Lady Penelope's FAB1

Dinky's first edition Thunderbird 2 came in a wonderful card box that could be used as a display stand.

Dinky wanted to fend off its arch rival Corgi Toys with some innovative *Thunderbirds* diecast toys with plenty of play features.

and Thunderbird 2. The reason behind this change of heart is likely to have been two-fold: firstly Anderson's shows were becoming increasingly popular so demand for toys was high and, secondly, Dinky's big diecast rival Corgi Toys was having fantastic success with its TV and film offerings.

In 1965 Corgi Toys released No. 261, James Bond's Aston Martin DB5, a toy that, just like the spy who inspired it, was absolutely packed with gadgets and features. There was an ejector seat allowing kids to catapult a plastic figure skywards from the passenger seat, a retractable bullet-proof screen, hidden machine guns and a rotating number plate. It was a revolution in the diecast world and was awarded 'Toy of Year' in 1965. Bond's DB5 went on to sell almost four million units before it was withdrawn in 1969 ... that's almost a million units a year!

However, it wasn't a flash in the pan because the following year lightning struck again for Corgi with its new Batmobile (No. 267), inspired by the 1966 live-action *Batman* television show. Once again, Corgi upped the ante and the diecast Batmobile included plastic figures of the Dynamic Duo, rotating 'flame' turbine at the rear, firing missiles and a disc cutter at the front. The Batmobile went on to become one of Corgi's most famous products, selling almost five million units before it was withdrawn in 1979.

Keen not to be outdone, Dinky turned its attentions to the small screen and in 1967 launched its first TV and film release: No. 100, Lady Penelope's FAB1. Finished in bright pink, like its larger cousin, the FAB1 also competed

A closer look at the Dinky example of Thunderbird 2 shows how the little plastic legs can be extended to allow the pod to drop down.

with Corgi's innovative releases with a number of stellar features, including a hidden missile that could be shot from a secret compartment behind the grille, four harpoons that are fired from the rear and plastic figures of Lady Penelope and her loyal butler Parker. Even the box aped the Corgi releases by turning into an impressive display stand, similar to the Aston Martin DB5. Compared to Dinky's often rather conservative releases, FAB1 with its shocking pink finish was a remarkable new product and is now very sought after with prices around the £200 mark for decent examples, although fluorescent pink examples can be worth double that.

However, Dinky wasn't finished with *Thunderbirds* and the same year it released No. 101, Thunderbird 2 and 4. The iconic craft from the show is turned into an equally impressive diecast replica that's the most famous of all Dinky's TV and film output. The shape of the real thing is captured perfectly and, here's the most exciting part, it features a removable cargo pod just like the version seen on the show. By popping down some extendable plastic legs, the cargo pod could be ejected, then opened up to reveal a tiny Thunderbird 4 inside! The only sad thing about Dinky's release is that, disappointingly, it never produced any of the different pods that could be fitted inside Thunderbird 2, but that's really a small grumble. Another slight grumble is that although Dinky did produce Thunderbird 2 in the dark green audiences had become accustomed to, it also made a metallic blue version. Understandably it's now the green version that tends to command the most when sold, with prices over £500 for mint examples, while the metallic blue edition trades for less than half that.

A later example of Lady Penelope's FAB1 came in a see-through blister pack, rather than the classic card one.

Dinky had hit upon something very special with the *Thunderbirds* diecast toys and, as we'll see later, this wasn't the only time Anderson and Dinky worked together.

Corgi Toys

In an ironic twist, Dinky's great rival Corgi Toys actually produced its own *Thunderbirds* diecast toys for the fortieth anniversary of the show in 2004. Just like Dinky, Corgi made FAB1 and Thunderbird 2, although advances in diecast production meant that the overall design of these later toys is actually slightly better than their 1960s counterparts. What's more, the features of the later models are identical to those of their predecessors, so FAB1 has the hidden missiles while Thunderbird 2 has the removable pod, complete with a gorgeous little Thunderbird 4.

Corgi Toys produced its own versions of FAB1 and Thunderbird 2 for the fortieth anniversary of the show.

Century 21

Thunderbirds also provided another interesting development in the world of Anderson toys, with new products from a company called Century 21. Now if that name sounds familiar it's because it was the logo seen before episodes of Anderson's later shows, such as *Captain Scarlet and the Mysterons*. However, the branding actually dates back further than that to the days before *Thunderbirds*. You see, along with running Anderson's production company AP Films, he also had his finger in plenty of other pies under the 'Century 21' name. There was Century 21 Publications, which produced comics inspired by his work, Century 21 Music, which released the soundtracks and audio books from the shows, and, finally, Century 21 Toys. AP Films itself was later rebranded to Century 21 Productions after the first episodes of *Thunderbirds* were shown.

Here, it's the Century 21 Toys that provide an area of interest. Produced by J. Rosenthal (Toys) Limited, the line of toys was initially known as JR21 but, in a similar vein to AP Films, the series became known as Century 21 Toys. Rosenthal manufactured a great line-up of toys inspired by *Thunderbirds* including typical entries like replicas of Thunderbirds 1 through 5 and FAB1, along with slightly more unusual items like water pistols and even a Lady Penelope-inspired jewellery set. The toys are among the best Anderson-themed collectables available and even made an appearance on-screen in the final ever episode of *Thunderbirds:* 'Give or Take a Million'.

J. R. Rosenthal made some spectacular Gerry Anderson toys, like this wonderful large-scale plastic Thunderbird 1.

Let's start with Thunderbird 1, which was available in both friction motor and battery-operated versions. The plastic friction motor variation is the smaller of the two, with wheels on the undercarriage and wings that can be manually moved into position. Meanwhile, the slightly bigger battery-operated replica came with the ability to move backwards or forwards. Unlike the friction-powered edition, here the wings would spring out when the nose cone was pressed, plus it had lights that came on and off during movement.

Thunderbird 2 only came in a friction-powered format, but what it lacks in battery power it makes up for with a removable cargo pod. In a similar fashion to the smaller Dinky version, four legs could be manually lowered to allow the removal of the pod which contained either a plastic version of the Mole or a Jeep ... there's sadly no Thunderbird 4 here, but the Mole is a decent addition; the Jeep not so much. Thunderbird 3 is a fairly simple friction-powered offering with no features, although Rosenthal absolutely nailed the distinctive appearance of the craft.

Thunderbird 4, meanwhile, gets the full battery-operated treatment and, incredibly for a battery-operated toy, can be safely operated on land and in water. That's right – a propeller on the plastic sub allows it to speed along on top of some water, allowing you to recreate your favourite International Rescue missions in the bath. Then, back on land, the battery-powered motor allowed it to drive along the carpet too. Inside Thunderbird 4 a small plastic version of Gordon Tracy can be seen sitting behind the controls. This truly is a spectacular *Thunderbirds* toy and is certainly among the most impressive Anderson-themed collectables we've seen and, as such, can be worth as much as £200 with the box and in mint, working condition.

Along with a friction-powered version, Rosenthal also released a remote control Thunderbird 1.

Thunderbird 2 has become one of the most iconic Gerry Anderson vehicles and Century 21's replica is spot-on.

Another friction-powered toy from Century 21 and Rosenthal, this time based on Thunderbird 3.

Thunderbird 4 is Rosenthal's most impressive *Thunderbirds* toy because it can be used on dry land and on the water. An absolute joy!

From underwater (well, on the water) to Earth's orbit now, with the battery-operated Thunderbird 5, which featured something called 'mystery action'. This was a term used on lots of toys throughout the 1960s and plenty of tinplate space toys from Japan featured this exotic-sounding function. In practice the 'mystery action' just meant the toy moved around in an unpredictable pattern once switched on. Along with the 'mystery action', Rosenthal's Thunderbird 5 featured a series of brightly coloured flashing lights. Ultimately, though, this particular Thunderbird 5 looks more like a UFO than the real thing, but it's still a fun little piece.

Although it doesn't look much like Thunderbird 5, this battery operated toy had plenty of fun play features.

Apart from Thunderbird 1, Lady Penelope's FAB1 was the only other vehicle to get the friction-powered and battery-operated treatment. In the friction versions, hidden guns eject from behind the grille by pressing a switch on the base of the vehicle. Meanwhile, the battery-operated edition uses the same mould but is crammed with features, including forward/reverse movement, wheels that could be locked into position to allow it to 'steer', headlights that come on when the car moves and the same hidden guns. In both versions, plastic figures of Lady Penelope and Parker are seen in the interior.

Century 21 made friction-powered and battery-powered examples of Lady Penelope's iconic FAB1.

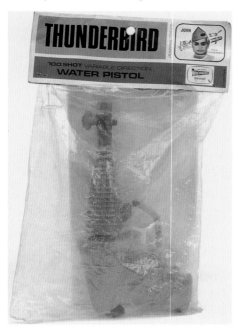

Along with the vehicles, Century 21 also released a series of different water guns and cap pistols.

As stated earlier, Rosenthal didn't just produce vehicles and the company also had a number of other products up its commercial sleeve. One of those was a rather neat red plastic water pistol that resembles the on-screen *Thunderbirds* weapons fairly well. It was packaged in a simple see-through bag with cardboard header featuring a picture of John Tracy. Rosenthal also produced a pair of plastic cap guns, available in either green or blue, with a picture of Scott Tracy on the card header this time. These aren't the last toys we'll see from Rosenthal, however, and the prolific manufacturer will return in our next chapter on *Captain Scarlet*.

Fairylite Thunderbirds

The 1960s proved to be a fertile time for the creation of new toys, thanks in part to manufacturing developments in plastic toys. One of the more innovative toys of the 1960s came in 1964 after Hasbro developed the G.I. Joe range of 12-inch action figures. Compared to the smaller action figures we're used to today, these large figures resembled – shock horror – dolls, but they were intended for boys rather than girls. Initially it must have been a hard sell to persuade boys to play with 'dolls', but G.I. Joe, 'America's Moveable Fighting Man', proved to be a huge success and even spawned its own British equivalent known as Action Man! That's right, one of Britain's biggest toy brands was actually born in America.

The Fairylite Thunderbirds have become highly sought after in later years as it's thought they weren't great sellers when first released.

Action Man wasn't the only toy inspired by G.I. Joe's success and British firm Fairylite created its own range of action figures – cough, dolls, cough – bearing the likenesses of the Tracy brothers. Released around the same time as Palitoy's Action Man's debut in the UK, the Fairylite Thunderbirds measured 12 inches, the same as their all-action counterparts. Fairylite produced ten characters in total: Scott, Virgil, Alan, Gordon, John, Jeff, Brains, Parker, Lady Penelope and Tin-Tin. All the males used the same fully-jointed bodies that could be put in 'any action position' according to the box while the ladies, as you would expect, had suitably feminine shapes.

Just like on the show, the Tracy brothers all wore blue cloth 'jump suit' style clothing with an appropriately coloured sash across their bodies. They also came with a neat blue hat, pin badge and gun, which was remarkably close to the weapon seen on-screen. Jeff, meanwhile, came in more appropriate casual wear including the essential 1960s bright orange polo neck jumper and beige suit ... very classy. Brains also had a different outfit, featuring the iconic thick glasses, lab coat and some suitably scientific accessories including a pencil, spanner and pliers. Finally for the men, we have Parker in his chauffeur outfit, including hat and long overcoat.

The Fairylite Thunderbirds are certainly among the rarest items covered so far and that could be because, although the idea of an action doll had caught on in the States thanks to G.I. Joe, over here in the UK the idea of a doll for boys wasn't quite the done thing. As a result, it's possible that Fairylite's Thunderbirds were innovative but ill-fated. To put their value in context, back in 2001 a set of six (Jeff, Virgil, Alan, John, Gordon and Scott), complete with their boxes and accessories, sold for £1,175. Even a few years later in 2007, Vectis sold a similar selection for £220 each!

Compared to their male colleagues, the females are a far classier affair, complete with some rather attractive 1960s clothing. 'Elegance charm and deadly danger' reads the packaging for Lady Penelope while she sports a natty checked dress, deerstalker hat and red cardigan. Fairylite even included some white knickers ... now, now everyone! Meanwhile, Tin-Tin (International Rescue's electronics expert) had a kimono (available in blue, red and gold) plus white kitten heels ... and those same knickers again. Arguably Fairylite had it wrong again because, although dolls are obviously more appropriate for girls, you've got to wonder whether they would have been bothered about watching *Thunderbirds*, which was a show aimed squarely at boys. It must have proved a conundrum at Fairylite HQ. In terms of value, both Lady Penelope and a red version of Tin-Tin sold at Vectis in 2015 for £120 and £130 respectively. Finally, for the sake of completeness, it's worth noting that Fairylite produced six different 'fashion' outfits for Lady Penelope: a blue ball gown, a kind of blue tracksuit, a black and white trouser suit, a black and white checked affair with red boots, a black roll neck with pink trousers and glasses and a kind of white trench coat. All very fetching, I'm sure you'll agree.

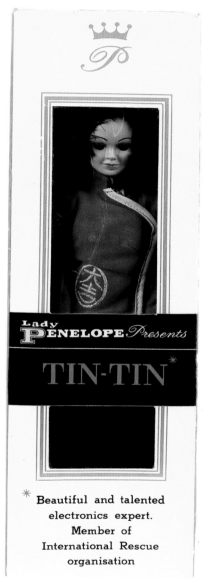

As well as the Tracy brothers, Fairylite also made a delightful Lady Penelope.

Lady Penelope was joined by her female pal Tin-Tin, International Rescue's electronics expert.

Captain Scarlet (1967/68)

After the worldwide success of *Thunderbirds*, following it up with a similarly successful show must have been a daunting task for Anderson and his production team. So, rather than create another colourful gang of do-gooders in their spectacular vehicles, Anderson took a slightly different approach with *Captain Scarlet and the Mysterons*.

From the opening credits it was clear this was a new approach for the team. The scene opens in a dark alley before Captain Scarlet appears and is seemingly shot to pieces by gunfire but manages to survive and shoots his aggressor with one shot. The high-pitched squeal of his victim is a clear indication Captain Scarlet has hit his target, possibly killing him. Yes, there were explosions galore in *Thunderbirds*, but this shout of pain is far more realistic than the over-the-top destruction of Anderson's previous work.

But that wasn't all. Next up, a chilling voice told us exactly how the Mysterons were going to exact their revenge in that particular episode. For example:

> This is the voice of the Mysterons, we know that you can hear us Earthmen. You attacked our complex on Mars and you will pay a heavy price. Our next act of retaliation will be to destroy the city of London. Do you hear Earthmen? We will destroy the city of London!

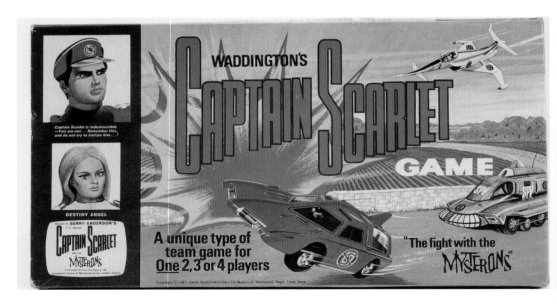

Despite the fact *Captain Scarlet* explored a darker tone, there are still plenty of toys bearing his image.

Compare that to the joyous 'Thunderbirds are go!' and you'll hopefully see we are in different territory with *Captain Scarlet*. Even the end credits set a different tone with images of the indestructible Captain Scarlet in a series of situations where he appears to be getting killed: drowning in a swamp, falling off a skyscraper, attacked by a giant snake, falling out of a moving vehicle, drowning while surrounded by sharks and crushed to death by spikes. All of these grim scenes are accompanied by a jolly upbeat 1960s song with lyrics like: 'They crash him and his body may burn. They smash him but they'll know he'll return to live again.' Seriously ... this is meant for kids?

Captain Scarlet also saw Anderson opt for a more realistic appearance for the puppets, adding to the sense of a more adult-themed show.

Anyway, concerns about the suitability for children aside, *Captain Scarlet* sees our titular hero and the elite Spectrum force fending off the advances of an alien invader called the Mysterons. In a plot twist that sounds like it came straight from *Invasion of the Body Snatchers*, when the seemingly invisible Mysterons kill an enemy they have the power to reanimate their corpse. One of their most notorious tools of espionage is Captain Black, the Spectrum agent who led the accidental attack on the Mysterons' Mars complex and has now become their representative on Earth.

Captain Scarlet is joined by other members of Spectrum, who are headquartered at the Cloudbase, situated 40,000 feet above Earth. Each agent of Spectrum is assigned a particular colour, so along with Captain Scarlet, there is also Colonel White, the Commander-in-Chief, Captain Blue, Lieutenant Green, Captain Magenta, Doctor Fawn and, well, you get the idea. Along with this colourful cast, Cloudbase was defended by a fleet of Angel Interceptor planes piloted by the Angels, five female pilots called Harmony, Melody, Destiny, Rhapsody and Symphony. As you would expect by now, Spectrum also had a host of high-tech vehicles at its disposal along with the Angel Interceptors, including the Spectrum Pursuit Vehicles and Spectrum Patrol Cars.

Century 21 Toys Zero-X

It's worth starting the *Captain Scarlet* selection with something rather unusual: the five-toys-in-one Zero-X spaceship. The toy itself, although spectacular, isn't the unusual thing; instead it's the back story behind the vehicle. You see, up until the arrival of Zero-X it was assumed, but not official, that there must be some crossover between the various worlds of Gerry Anderson's output. After all, there are only a couple of years between *Stingray, Thunderbirds* and *Captain Scarlet*.

Zero-X is the only vehicle that officially appears in a number of different Anderson works: the *Thunderbirds* movie (*Thunderbirds Are Go!*), *Captain Scarlet* and a comic series called *Project SWORD*. In *Thunderbirds Are Go!* Zero-X takes part in an ill-fated mission to Mars after the villainous Hood sabotaged the ship and the crew had to be saved by International Rescue. The spaceship is then recomissioned by Spectrum, where it then takes part in another ill-fated mission and this time ends up accidentally destroying the Mysteron base. Talk about bad luck!

The toy inspired by this doomed craft is, thankfully, more impressive. The large metallic blue toy is controlled via a remote control that resembles a walkie-talkie, allowing it to go forwards and backwards. Various parts of the ship can be detached to create separate smaller vehicles like the Martian Exploration Vehicle (MEV), two smaller

Zero-X is the only vehicle that officially links the worlds of *Thunderbirds* and *Captain Scarlet*.

spaceships and the detachable nose cone, similar to an escape pod. Sadly all these detachable parts means that sections of the Zero-X often get lost, so it's a rare beast to find complete and in its box.

On the subject of Zero-X, Japanese company Aoshima released a very impressive diecast version of the spacecraft in 2006. Rather like the Century 21 version, it's become very sought after, with prices up to £200 on eBay for mint in box examples.

Become a member of Spectrum with this nifty *Captain Scarlet* badge from Lone Star.

More Century 21 Toys

After Rosenthal had begun producing Anderson-themed toys under the Century 21 moniker for *Thunderbirds*, it continued to manufacture some extremely impressive large-scale plastic vehicles inspired by *Captain Scarlet* too.

First up is the Spectrum Pursuit Vehicle (SPV), the heavily armoured tank that Captain Scarlet and the team use as their main attack vehicle on the ground. Bizarrely, the crew actually sit backwards when driving and use video screen technology to see where they're going. Arguably a little pointless, but it must have seemed exceptionally high tech in the 1960s. That aside, Rosenthal's take on the spectacular SPV is wonderful with not four but TEN wheels, an ejector seat in the roof and missiles. However, although the real thing was extremely rugged, the toy tends to be more fragile, so watch out for snapped off aerials and broken hatches.

Along with the SPV, Rosenthal also made Captain Scarlet's main vehicle of choice: the Spectrum Patrol Car. Although lacking the numerous play features of the SPV, this large-scaled friction-powered toy still looks wonderful thanks to a bright red finish and gleaming chrome wheels. Meanwhile, a basic replica of Captain Scarlet himself is seen sitting behind the wheel. One thing to watch out for with the Patrol Car is that it came with a selection of tiny plastic accessories (rear fin, radio, Mysteron detector, suitcase and spare missiles) that invariably get lost – something to bear in mind if you're after a mint example.

Rosenthal's Spectrum Pursuit Vehicle is spectacular, as is the brightly coloured eye-catching packaging.

Along with the Spectrum Pursuit Vehicle, Rosenthal made an equally impressive Spectrum Patrol Car in bright red plastic.

Finally from Rosenthal/Century 21 is the Angel Aircraft, as piloted by the Angels in the show. The unusual shape of the dart-like interceptor is captured beautifully in the toy and its sleek, angular lines look like they've come straight out of the show ... although that pointy nose probably would be seen as a little dangerous today. Features included a removable friction motor, firing missiles and ejecting pilot figure. It's a gorgeous but extremely delicate toy with plenty of spindly parts that could easily be snapped off.

The pointy shape of the Angel Aircraft certainly makes for an unusual appearance.

Dinky Toys

Another firm favourite returns for *Captain Scarlet* in the form of Dinky, which released three diecast vehicles from the show: No. 103 Spectrum Patrol Car, No. 104 Spectrum Pursuit Vehicle and No. 105 Maximum Security Vehicle. All three were produced between 1968 and 1975 and there are numerous colour variations for each to look out for.

Starting with the Spectrum Patrol Car, Dinky really tried to push the boundaries with this one by including 'real' engine noise as the toy was pressed downwards. 'First again!' boasted the box: 'Jet engine sound'. The noise was more like a high-pitched screech than a jet engine, but it must have added some excitement to play times. Still, the toy itself is a real beaut and looks like it's driven straight off the *Captain Scarlet* set, particularly the metallic red version. Dinky released a number of variations of the Spectrum Patrol Cars and there are examples finished in red, metallic red and metallic gold, plus reports of metallic blue and silver versions, although according to the *Ramsay's Guide to British Diecast* these have yet to be seen 'in the wild'. Value wise it's the metallic red version that's the most sought after and one sold at Vectis Auctions in 2014 for £340.

Dinky returned for *Captain Scarlet* with numerous diecast vehicles inspired by the show, like this Spectrum Patrol Car.

Along with a metallic red version, Dinky Toys also released a metallic bronze edition.

Next up, the No. 104 Spectrum Pursuit Vehicle also saw Dinky trying to out-do the competition at Corgi with some excellent play features, including an opening front hatch with firing missile, rubber front bumper, drop-down rubber tracks at the rear, folding roof aerial and a special side door that opens up to reveal a seated Captain Scarlet figure. It's a joy to play with and shows that Dinky really was trying to push the envelope with its Anderson offerings. Once again there are various finishes and different packaging for the SPV, but the most valuable is the original metallic blue version in a card picture box with display stand, with a value around the £250 mark.

Dinky's Spectrum Pursuit Vehicle was one of its most innovative releases and is a beautiful replica of the on-screen vehicle.

Finally from Dinky is No. 105 Maximum Security Vehicle and, sadly, this is the poor relation to the other two models. Ultimately, although accurate to the show, the shape of the design and the lack of windows just means it looks a little like a white blob on wheels. Even the inclusion of a folding ramp, complete with plastic box of 'radioactive isotopes', can't help this one.

Sadly, compared to Dinky's other *Captain Scarlet* models, the Maximum Security Vehicle looks rather drab.

Tri-ang Captain Scarlet Spectrum Patrol Cars

Along with Dinky and Corgi, another of the big diecast names in the 1960s was Tri-ang and its Spot-On range of vehicles. Although Tri-ang tended to stick to 'real' road cars, rather than the imaginary vehicles seen on the small screen, it did produce a handful of TV and film-related toys featuring the likes of Batman and, you guessed it, Captain Scarlet.

Tri-ang's Magicars featured a special function that saw them speed across the floor after the sides of the vehicles were pressed.

Along with a double pack, Tri-ang also released a single Spectrum Patrol Car in a blister pack.

However, rather than being made of diecast, Tri-ang's offerings were so-called 'Magicars'. These 'magic cars' had interchangeable bodies and a motor that could be operated by pressing the sides of the vehicle, which would send it zooming off. Tri-ang produced two sets featuring the Spectrum Patrol Car. First is the *Captain Scarlet* two-car set with '21st Century Auto-highway' and 'Touch-to-Drive Patrol Vehicles', which comes with models finished in yellow and red, plus a slot car-style track for the cars to drive around. Tri-ang also made a single car set featuring just the red Spectrum Patrol Car and some grey plastic track.

Pedigree Captain Scarlet Action Figure

If you'll cast your mind back to the previous chapter, you'll remember that Fairylite attempted to create one of the first Anderson 'action figures' with its *Thunderbirds* range. Sadly it seemed British boys weren't ready to play with 'dolls' in 1965 but by the time *Captain Scarlet* hit television screens in 1967, the country had gone action figure mad thanks to Palitoy's Action Man range.

So the time was right for another company to have a go at an Anderson action figure and doll company Pedigree certainly stepped up to the plate with its wonderful Captain Scarlet offering. Of course, Pedigree certainly had some, well, pedigree in this area after launching Sindy in 1966 along with its own 'doll for boys' called Tommy Gunn. Dressed in Second World War garb, Tommy was the classic British soldier, ready for action with his Sten gun, boots with real laces and a better level of articulation than his rival Action Man.

Pedigree's Captain Scarlet 'doll' is wonderful and was based on the Tommy Gunn action figure for boys.

Although Tommy Gunn was arguably the better toy than Palitoy's Action Man, it didn't have the same success and was withdrawn in 1968. That same year, however, Pedigree had the foresight to reuse the Tommy Gunn body moulds to create a Captain Scarlet figure and the result was extremely impressive. Captain Scarlet comes with a hat (complete with radio microphone), zip-up red jacket, belt, plastic boots and even a gun that he can hold. The Pedigree Captain Scarlet has become one of the most sought after Captain Scarlet toys because it was rumoured to have only been produced in small numbers (perhaps to use up the remaining Tommy Gunn bodies) and the accessories are easily lost. To give you some idea of its scarcity, Vectis Auction has only sold four in the past fifteen years and the last example made £440. Meanwhile, on eBay, the gun alone sells for around £60!

Before moving on, it's worth mentioning that Pedigree also produced bendable dolls of both Captain Scarlet and Destiny Angel. Made of rubber, the figures could be posed in different positions thanks to the bendy material. Although the Destiny example does sometimes crop up at auction, the Captain Scarlet example is exceptionally scarce with eBay throwing up one of the only known examples back in 2012.

Captain Scarlet and the Spectrum crew were even turned into toy soldiers, courtesy of toy figure manufacturer Timpo.

Joe 90 (1968/69)

While *Captain Scarlet* saw Anderson adopting a more realistic style with the puppet design and a more serious tone with the dark plots of alien invasion, *Joe 90* once again saw a shift in focus. Gone were the global rescue agencies of WASP or International Rescue; instead *Joe 90* told the adventures of the schoolboy.

Of course, that nine-year-old schoolboy just happens to be a super spy who can absorb untold amounts of knowledge thanks to an invention called the BIG RAT (Brain Impulse Galvanoscope Record and Transfer). Created by his adopted father Professor Ian 'Mac' McClaine, the BIG RAT allows Joe to 'download' knowledge from experts in their chosen field, for example brain surgery, and then immediately learn that skill.

The benefits of this incredible technology are quickly spotted by the World Intelligence Network (WIN), which enlists Joe to become its Most Special Agent. Joe then becomes a kind of mini James Bond, traveling around the globe thwarting criminals or terrorist threats. Before each mission Joe would be required to use the BIG RAT to gather the necessary knowledge before donning his special thick-rimmed glasses, known as 'electrode glasses', to trigger the information.

Rather like *Captain Scarlet*, *Joe 90* continued to explore more adult themes and was less spectacular than shows like *Thunderbirds*.

Dress just like Joe 90, courtesy of these bizarre slip-on shoes.

Dinky Toys

We're back on familiar territory with *Joe 90* as the majority of the best *Joe 90*-themed toys were produced by Dinky Toys, Century 21 and Pedigree. Dinky had two releases up its sleeve for *Joe 90*, namely No. 102 Joe's Car and No. 108 Sam's Car. Sam's Car was last manufactured in 1971, while Joe's Car lasted a little bit longer and went out of production in 1975.

Joe's Car is certainly the more impressive of the two releases, thanks mainly to its spectacular appearance in the show. The 'Jet Air Car', to give it its full name, is an invention of Professor McClaine and, rather like Supercar, the vehicle is capable of driving at 200 mph on land, traveling on water as a hovercraft and was equipped with retractable wings that allowed it to fly. It looks like nothing else from Anderson's previous work and is a bizarre mix of bubble car and jet engine. Dinky's take on the strange car certainly captures the design of McClaine's invention and even includes a few innovative play features such as automatic opening wings, extending tail fins, independent suspension and a battery-powered light-up jet turbine, making it one of the few Dinky toys to require a battery. It was certainly an impressive feat of manufacturing to replicate that bonkers shape.

Dinky certainly managed to capture the strange shape of Joe 90's Jet Air Car.

Meanwhile, Sam's Car was more pedestrian in appearance compared to the outlandish vehicle driven by Joe, resembling a fairly typical sports car rather than a science experiment. The big feature of Dinky's replica was the fact it was: 'Motorised with new powerful keyless clockwork motor', another first for Dinky. The keyless clockwork motor worked by pulling the vehicle backwards and then, once let go, it would speed off into the distance. Apart from that though, play features were in short supply for Sam. Perhaps the most interesting aspect of Dinky's Sam's Car is the numerous variations in colour, some of which are more scarce than others. Despite the fact the car is shown as silver in the television show, Dinky produced examples in chrome, gold, pale blue, metallic red and dark red. Out of those colours it's the pale blue that's the most rare and is worth around £200, compared to £100 for the chrome finish ... in good condition, of course.

Compared to Joe's car, Sam's vehicle of choice looked more like a typical sports car.

Dinky made Sam's Car in a number of different colours, including this light blue example.

Century 21 Joe 90 toys

Another regular makes an appearance with its *Joe 90* replicas, as Century 21/Rosenthal throws its hat into the ring. Just like Dinky, Century 21 made both the Jet Air Car and Sam's Car. There really wasn't much choice when it came to *Joe 90* vehicles, unlike Anderson's previous work. The Jet Air Car came in two forms: friction-powered and battery-powered with a remote, similar to the FAB1 and Thunderbird 1 toys Century 21 had already produced.

Century 21's Jet Air Car is perfect and must have been a great treat for children in the 1960s.

The remote control version is the more impressive with numerous features including forward and reverse movement, retractable tail fins, automatic extending wings and headlights. All very exciting! The remote control also resembles the undeniably cool 'walkie talkie' appearance already seen on Century 21's Zero-X. Meanwhile, clocking in at a fairly large 12 inches, the friction-powered car has automatic retractable wings that pop out when the turbine engines are pressed.

Century 21/Rosenthal also made a remote controlled battery-powered version of Joe's famous car.

Similar to the Dinky replica of Sam's Car, the Century 21 version looks like a typical sports car.

Sadly Sam only gets a friction-powered car and it's much smaller than Joe's, measuring around 7 inches. Even worse, it doesn't have a great deal of features, unless an opening bonnet and spring suspension really float your boat. All the Century 21 vehicles tend to sell for around £100, depending upon the condition.

However, along with the vehicles, Century 21 also produced a number of suitably spy-themed gadgets and accessories for wannabe Joes to use while out in the field. From miniature guns to those famous glasses, Century 21 made sure any young spy would be appropriately tooled up.

Pedigree Joe 90

After producing the superlative Captain Scarlet in 1968, Pedigree returned with its take on Joe. Measuring 6 inches, almost half the height of his predecessor, Pedigree's Joe 90 is a bit of a mixed bag in terms of accuracy. Yes, it does come with some fetching thick black glasses, a red leatherette-style suit, tiny shoes and a WIN badge, but the appearance of Joe himself leaves a lot to be desired. Firstly he appears to be wearing pink lipstick, has long eye lashes and has a hair-do that's more super model than super spy. Overall then, not Pedigree's best work.

After Pedigree's stellar work on Captain Scarlet, its take on Joe 90 is ... well ... different. Those eyelashes are rather fetching though.

Lone Star Joe 90 Walkie-Talkie Two Way Radio

Let's finish off on something far more spy-like, with Lone Star's cracking walkie-talkie. Although radio communication like this is nothing new – Merit was doing it with Supercar back in the 1950s – the packaging and presentation for this set elevate it to another level. The car box opens up to reveal Joe chatting away to what appears to be Shane Weston on the lid. 'Send and receive without batteries!' blasts the box, basically hiding the fact that these, really, are glorified tin cans with strings attached. Still, at least the walkie-talkies included a 'secret high frequency whistle' and 'extending aerial', although why anyone needed an aerial for these wired communication devices is anyone's guess.

This is far more like it: Lone Star's walkie-talkies came in a super card box, although the actual toys are glorified tin cans!

Joe 90 had some fairly graphic violence, which caused a bit of a stir at the time, so it should come as no surprise to hear Lone Star produced a range of weapons.

Along with the walkie-talkies, Lone Star was on more familiar territory with its *Joe 90* Repeater Cap Pistol, which looked like a fairly typical gun but with 'Joe 90' emblazoned on the hilt. The pistols came with an optional silencer and Lone Star also made a natty white holster to hold them in.

Along with the futuristic toys, Joe 90 also appeared on more traditional products, like these jigsaws showing images from the show.

The Secret Service (1969)

A brief mention now for Gerry Anderson's final Supermarionation series *The Secret Service*, which was launched in September 1969 but was quickly pulled in December that year after only thirteen episodes! *The Secret Service* was unusual in that it used puppets for close-up shots and actual actors for other scenes. The story centres around Father Stanley Unwin who is a member of the British Intelligence's secret BISHOP (British Intelligence Service Headquarters, Operation Priest) agency. The show is similar to *Joe 90*, with its themes of espionage and threats of terrorist attacks, along with high-tech gadgets like the Minimiser, which can shrink Unwin's assistant Matthew Harding, enabling him to go on secret reconnaissance missions. Compared to Anderson's previous work featuring daring rescue, intergalactic travel and underwater combat, the quaint British village setting and the bizarre concept of a secret agent pretending to be a priest must have seemed sadly rather pedestrian.

Rather like the series, Dinky's *The Secret Service* diecast replica is a curiosity.

The short run of *The Secret Service* means that toys are in very short supply and only one really stands out: Dinky's No. 109 Gabriel's Model T Ford, which was only produced between 1969 and 1971 – another indication of the show's failure to capture imaginations. The toy really sums up what was wrong with the show because there are no gadgets, no impressive features, no noises, no friction motors ... no excitement! It's literally just a black and yellow Model T with a figure of Father Unwin; a kid getting this in Christmas 1969 would have wondered what the heck was going on. From a toy point of view, *The Secret Service* is best forgotten as a curious blip.

UFO (1970/71)

After thirteen years of working with puppets, *UFO* marked a huge departure for Gerry Anderson because he started to work with actual actors rather than marionettes. That's right – no strings, no lip-synching and no problems walking around the set! However, what *UFO* lacked in puppets, it certainly made up for in special effects, something Anderson had been working on since first making *Twizzle* back in 1957.

UFO toys are in short supply – probably because this was the first Gerry Anderson show aimed squarely at adults.

UFO also marked another important turning point for Gerry Anderson because it was aimed squarely at adults rather than children. While *Captain Scarlet* and even *Joe 90* had dabbled with more adult themes, *UFO* went the whole hog with plots centred around divorce, drug use, murder and an alien race that is attacking Earth to harvest human organs. *UFO* was a million miles away from Zoonie the alien from *Fireball XL5*! Still, although this was unlike anything we had seen from Gerry Anderson, it still featured a fun acronym with SHADO (Supreme Headquarters, Alien Defence Organisaton), so there was still some familiar ground.

This unusual board game is among a handful of *UFO* tie-ins.

Dinky Toys

Due to the fact that *UFO* was a more adult-oriented series there wasn't a great deal of merchandise released around the show's original broadcast in 1970 but, luckily, our old friends at Dinky made sure there were at least some diecast models inspired by the show. In 1971 Dinky released No. 351 UFO Interceptor, No. 352 Ed Straker's Car and No. 353 SHADO 2 Mobile – the Interceptor and SHADO 2 Mobile had a great run and were in production for around eight years, while Ed Straker's motor of choice didn't fair quite as well and was pulled in 1975.

The No. 351 UFO Interceptor is based on the 'moon-based attack vehicle' that regularly appears in the show. The unusually shaped craft has a huge missile at the front, which is used to destroy any invading UFOs, while on the undercarriage it appears to have ski-like landing gear – a kind of combination between Joe 90's Jet Air Car and the Angel Interceptors. Fair play to Dinky, though, who got the shape just right in its 1971 replica, though it failed miserably when it came to the colour. In the show we saw a white/grey version, but Dinky opted for a striking metallic green finish, while the landing gear was bright orange or red. Still, a nice touch was the fact the over-sized missile allowed for a cap to be placed inside, ensuring it went with a real bang when fired.

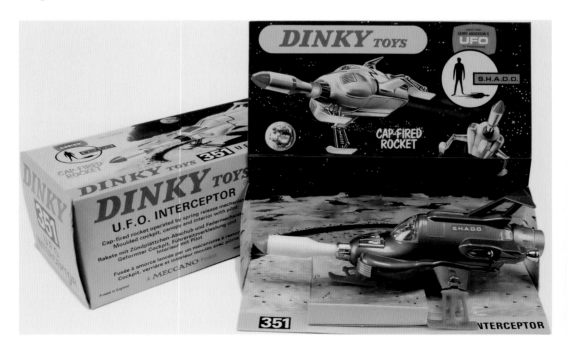

Dinky's latest innovation was a huge missile that include a cap-firing function.

Like Dinky's version of Sam's Car from *Joe 90*, Ed Straker's motor was fashioned in a number of different colours.

Along with yellow, Dinky also made this eye-catching golden edition.

Meanwhile No. 352 Ed Straker's Car suffered a similar problem to Sam's Car from *Joe 90*, in that it didn't really have much in the way of features. Rather than creating something new, Dinky opted to use the keyless clockwork motor from Sam's Car too. Perhaps the most intriguing thing about Dinky's *UFO* car is that it was one of the vehicles moulded in plastic for a proposed budget range from Dinky. In 1980 Dinky made several pre-production plastic models for the 'Low Price Point Range' and among the more typical trucks and cars, Ed Straker's Car was one of the options considered. An example was sold at Vectis Auctions as part of the Peter Allen Archive Dinky Collection in 2004 and made £700.

UFO did, however, inspire one of Dinky's best diecast replicas. The Shado 2 Mobile was jam-packed with great features.

Although the Shado 2 Mobile is off-white in the show, the military green version doesn't look out of place and would look great as an Earth army vehicle!

Finally from Dinky is the No. 353 SHADO 2 Mobile and this is a real winner. In terms of Dinky diecast offerings it's up there with Thunderbird 2 and the Spectrum Patrol Car. This extremely rugged toy has flexible rubber tracks, just like a tank, and a hatch that flips round to reveal a hidden missile. Even better, the rocket can be rotated 360 degrees to fire in any direction so that no alien invaders are safe! This is a beast of a toy and, although the series may not have been aimed at kids, this cracking science fiction vehicle must have been a real hit with children in the 1970s. In the *UFO* show, the SHADO 2 is, once again, a kind of grey/white colour but, never one to stick to a colour palette, Dinky produced a military-style olive green version and an eye-catching metallic blue edition. *UFO* may not have inspired many toys but Dinky's SHADO 2 is a worthy legacy.

Space: 1999 (1975–77)

Following the serious science fiction of *UFO*, Gerry Anderson followed it up with *Space: 1999* – a series that actually began life as the second series of *UFO*. However, when the second season was scrapped Anderson used a lot of the preliminary work to create an entirely new series set on the Moon. The first episode details how the Moon is shot out of orbit by a group of technologically advanced aliens and ends up drifting around deep space. In a similar vein to *Star Trek*, the crew of Moonbase Alpha drifted through space on the Moon encountering all manners of alien life. In another similarity to *Star Trek*, in the second season of the show an advanced alien life form known as Maya tags along for the ride, offering a different view on humanity's efforts to fine a new home.

After *UFO*, Gerry Anderson returned to space once more with the cult classic *Space: 1999*.

This Stun Gun by BBRB is a super replica of the on-screen gun and has various coloured lights that would light up when operated.

The two seasons of *UFO* have some quite stark contrasts, as the production team changed between the series. The first half is perhaps more 'British' in its approach with comparisons made to *Doctor Who*, while season two had more action and an American tone, like the hugely successful *Star Trek*. However, throughout both seasons, Anderson's eye for spectacular action sequences was certainly apparent.

Dinky Toys

That's right, you guessed it, Dinky was quick off the mark with two diecast models inspired by *Space: 1999* and both were released in 1975 – the same year *Space: 1999* was first broadcast. The first is No. 359 Eagle Transporter, produced until 1979, and the second is No. 360 Eagle Freighter. There really isn't a great deal of difference between the two, as both look a little like space scaffolding with a cockpit, boosters and landing gear attached. The white 'scaffolding' was made of plastic, while the extremities were diecast. In a similar vein to the fabulous Thunderbird 2, the Transporter featured a pod that could be ejected from the main canopy at the push of a button and the Freighter had six detachable atomic waster containers. The feet, meanwhile, were equipped with shock absorbers for those heavy impacts on planets.

Here's a superb shop display unit with both the Eagle Transporter and Eagle Freighter.

The Eagle Freighter came with six plastic yellow barrels that could be detached from the main ship.

Once again, Dinky's been a little liberal with the colour scheme, but it's still a very iconic spaceship.

However, once again, Dinky was a little liberal with the paint job, as seen with the UFO Interceptor, and instead of being off-white, the Dinky replica featured a bright green cockpit and landing gear. Then again, considering the rather pedestrian appearance of the Captain Scarlet Maximum Security Vehicle, perhaps Dinky felt it was necessary to give the toy a little colour to ensure it appealed to children.

Meanwhile, the Eagle Freighter was initially released in a predominantly white finish, apart from the red cargo-pod housing six yellow drums containing potentially lethal nuclear waste. The colour scheme was changed, though, and the diecast parts became a metallic blue, while the pod was changed to white. Fans might consider mixing the two versions to offer up a mostly all-white variation like that seen in the series.

Palitoy Space: 1999 Action Figures

Two years before Leicestershire company Palitoy would find international fame with its *Star Wars* action figures, it was dabbling in the world of science fiction figures thanks to *Space: 1999*. In 1975 Palitoy employed action figure experts Mego – who had created the incredibly successful series of World's Greatest Superhero figures featuring the likes of Batman, Spider-Man and Captain America – to make its own range of *Space: 1999* toys.

Whereas some of the World's Greatest Superheroes were often crude in their design – featuring the same bodies and simple costumes – Mego certainly went to town on its *Space: 1999* line with

85

differently moulded heads, detailed costumes and perfectly sculpted hair. It's likely that Palitoy had seen Mego's previous work on the *Star Trek* range (which Palitoy distributed in the UK) and thought a similar effect could be achieved with the *Space: 1999* figures.

British company Palitoy drafted in American giant Mego to create its range of *Space: 1999* action figures.

Mego had a long history of producing action figures, such as superheroes like Batman and characters from science fiction shows like *Planet of the Apes* and *Star Trek*.

Here's the full range of Palitoy's *Space: 1999* products.

Mego produced five toys: Alan Carter, Captain Koenig, Captain Zantor, the Mysterious Alien and Paul Morrow. Alan Carter is modeled in his bright red chief pilot costume complete with helmet, laser blaster and yellow belt, though the Palitoy catalogue from 1976 shows him in the more typical white Moonbase Alpha outfit. Captain Koenig (although he was actually Commander Koenig in the show) and Paul Morrow (who suffered an unexplained and untimely demise between the two seasons) are both modeled in their white Moonbase Alpha attire. The head sculpts of actors Martin Landau and Prentis Hancock, who played Koenig and Morrow respectively, are absolutely spot-on.

Along with the humans, Palitoy also released the alien Captain Zantor, who appeared in an episode of *Space: 1999* called 'Earthbound'. With his long flowing blonde/white locks, silver brows and long flowing outfit, Zantor is actually a pretty good likeness, despite being an alien. Finally, the remaining outer space figure is the appropriately named Mysterious Alien with a bulbous head and bright purple gown. The unnamed alien appears in an episode called 'Wargames' in which they attack Moonbase Alpha. Value-wise the aliens tend to be less popular than their human counterparts, with prices under £50 for boxed ones. However, boxed examples of Koenig in particular appear to be in vogue at the time of writing, as one sold for more than £400 on eBay.

Mattel

However, Mego wasn't the only American company producing *Space: 1999* toys. In 1976 toy giant Mattel released its own series of 9-inch action figures of Commander Koenig, Professor Bergman and Dr Russell. Perhaps the most charming thing about these figures is the gorgeously illustrated packaging, in which each different character gets their own shot at taking centre stage, complete with dramatic explosions and the moon behind them.

Palitoy had some competition for the *Space: 1999* action figure market, courtesy of Mattel.

To accompany the 9-inch line of figures, Mattel produced the 'Moon Base Alpha', which was a large-scale playset featuring a computer console with flashing lights, vinyl play mat, space furniture and scenery ... perfect for creating your own space dramas at home.

However, the most impressive of Mattel's *Space: 1999* offerings is the huge 77-cm-long Eagle 1 Spaceship that was big enough for smaller 5-inch figures of Koenig, Bergman and Russell to sit inside. The Command Module could be detached to create a separate spaceship and the hatch doors of the cargo bay could be opened to reveal the interior, which was also big enough for the figures to fit in. An absolutely stunning piece for any *Space: 1999* fan!

Mattel produced this superb large-scale plastic Eagle Transporter, complete with figures to sit inside the cockpit.

Considering *Space: 1999* was a show for adults, there is a surprising amount of toys inspired by the series.

Terrahawks (1983–86)

Our journey, which began back in 1957, comes to an end now in 1983. Rather appropriately, *Terrahawks* saw Gerry Anderson returning to his roots with a brand new puppet-based show. However, instead of potentially costly marionettes as used in the Supermarionation days, *Terrahawks* used latex hand puppets in a process dubbed Supermacronation.

Once again, Anderson is back on familiar territory with a group of brave heroes defending Earth against an alien threat using a selection of super high-tech vehicles. In a similar vein to the Japanese cartoon *Science Ninja Team Gatchaman* (known in the UK as *Battle of the Planets*), the Terrahawks had vehicles shaped like birds and even their names were bird-like, such as Captain Mary Falconer and Captain Kate Kestrel (who just happened to be an international pop star when she wasn't saving the world).

Terrahawks is almost one of the 'forgotten' shows by Gerry Anderson because it featured Supermacronation, rather than Supermarionation.

By the 1980s licensed products were extremely common, so manufacturers were queuing up to make *Terrahawks* toys.

Certainly compared to *Captain Scarlet* and *UFO*, the plots of *Terrahawks* were clearly aimed at children with plenty of humour provided by the evil alien Zelda and her dimwitted relatives Cy-Star and Yung-Star, along with a group of spherical robots called Zeroids, once of which was famously voiced by British actor Windsor Davies. Depending upon your age, *Terrahawks* is either one of the best or one of the worst series Anderson made. For those who remembered the marionettes of *Thunderbirds*, the tongue-in-cheek plots and latex puppets of *Terrahawks* must have seemed a step too far but for children who grew up in the 1980s, the superb vehicle designs, quirky cast and videogame-style graphics were a joy. As such, it is perhaps best described as a 'cult classic'.

Bandai Terrahawks

Although the Dinky diecast replicas of Thunderbird 2, FAB1, the Spectrum Patrol Vehicle, etc. were innovative and impressive for their time, in this author's opinion the best Anderson diecast (with a little bit of plastic thrown in for good measure) came courtesy of Japanese company Bandai and its superb *Terrahawks* Action Models range.

Bandai produced the Battlehawk, Terrahawk, Treehawk, Action Zeroid and Hawkwing as part of the deluxe Action Model series and each was absolutely jam-packed with play features. This was the 1980s so now toys had to compete with videogames, as well as other toy manufacturers.

The Battlehawk measured around 9 inches long and came with a small plastic Terrahawk spaceship that could be fired from the top of the model, a tiny replica of the Battletank in diecast that could be winched up using a 'recovery hook' and the rear cargo bay doors could open. The Terrahawk is certainly the most bird-like of the vehicles and the toy has missile launchers at the front, wings that can pivot and retractable landing gears that resemble bird's legs.

Bandai's diecast versions of the various vehicles from *Terrahawks* are superb with plenty of features for fun playtimes.

Although not that expensive to buy now, the prices for *Terrahawks* products are starting to increase as fans look to reclaim their old toys.

Next up is the Treehawk, which makes up for its rather pedestrian rocket-shaped appearance with some neat features, such as a nose cone that slides forward, retractable landing gear and firing missiles underneath the folding wings. Finally on the vehicle front is the exceedingly impressive Hawkwing, which is almost two toys in one. The top wing section, complete with firing missiles, detaches from the base unit to create two separate vehicles.

Although these deluxe toys are certainly the most impressive products made by Bandai, it didn't stop there and they also released smaller diecast/plastic versions of the vehicles with more basic play features. What's more, because the 1980s had seen a huge boom in the action figure market, courtesy of *Star Wars*, Bandai manufactured all the main characters as both 3-inch and three-quarter-inch action figures. It seems somewhat ironic that we're almost approaching 2020, the year in which *Terrahawks* is set, and now these 'modern' Gerry Anderson collectables are becoming more sought after – by 2020 they could be just as valuable as their earlier counterparts. It's testimony to the stellar work and creative genius of Gerry Anderson that even after all these years we're still talking about the amazing programmes he made and the equally amazing toys inspired by them.

Gerry Anderson's incredible works on iconic vehicles like Thunderbird 2 will continue to inspire generations to come.

Although our time is up, the shows made by Gerry Anderson and the toys inspired by them are timeless and will be collectable for years to come.